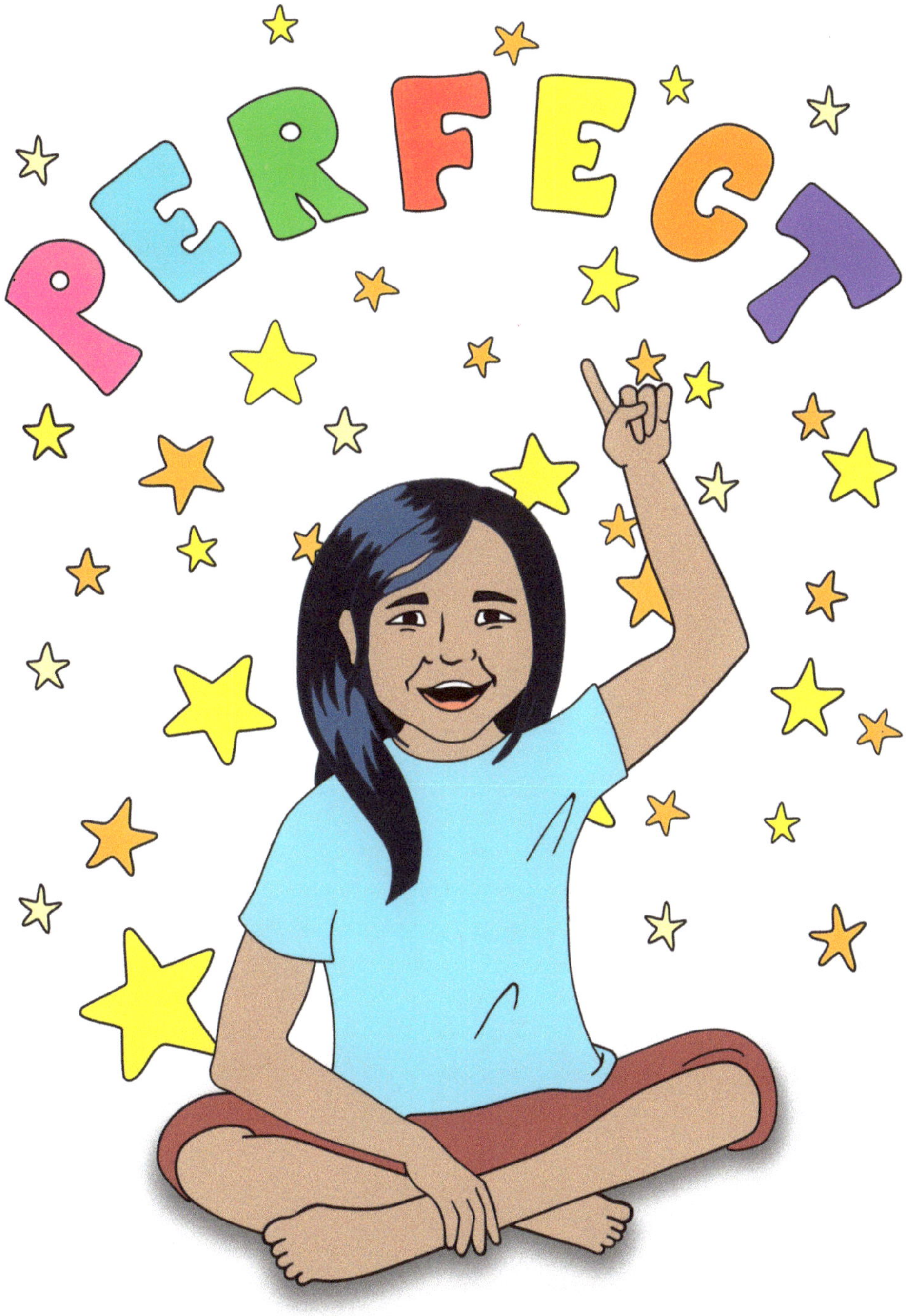

PERFECT

Written and illustrated by
Suzanne Wylde

for Emilia,

*Jumping in a puddle,
making a big splash!
Down for cuddlewuddles
and laughing in a flash.*

You can try some of the things in this book. When you see this star, why not join in?

Text and illustrations © 2021 Suzanne Wylde
Many Trees Publishing
ISBN: 978-1-8380352-4-2

www.suzannewylde.com

In our great big world, some things are always true.

Breathe in love, breathe out heavy feelings.

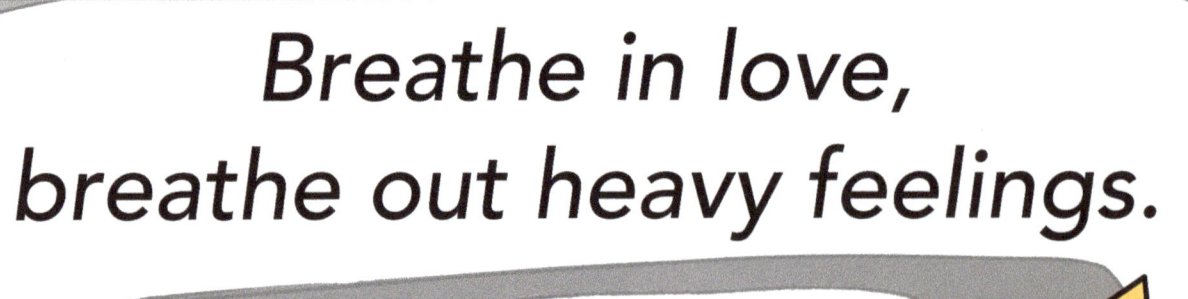

Try it with me

Some days I don't feel loving,

I feel some other things...

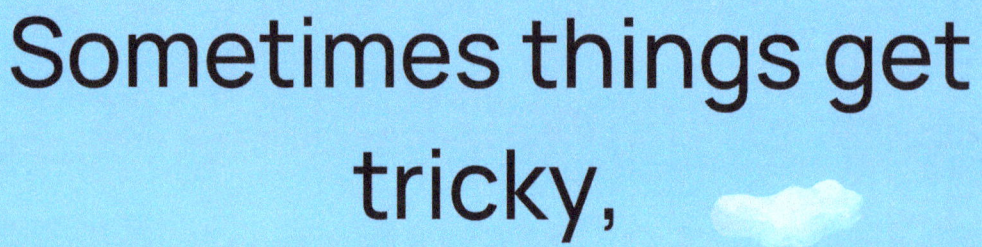

Sometimes things get tricky,

At these times I can remember, things are going to be OK...

So, however you are feeling, whether life is great or tough...

And in our perfect bodies,
full of life and full of love.

_____ is perfect!

Some of the words you may need to describe features of characters in this book include: disabled person, limb difference, cleft lip and palate, visually impaired, blind, Down syndrome and port wine stain. Please note these terms may vary at different times, in different countries and from person to person.

Some of the characters feel: happy, sad, disappointed, frustrated, overexcited, lonely, mean, excited, joyful, loving, excluded, included, calm, safe, free, confident, strong - how many feelings can you spot?

Copyright © 2021 Suzanne Wylde

Many Trees Publishing
ISBN: 978-1-8380352-4-2

All rights reserved. No part of this publication may be reproduced without prior written permission of the author.

The moral rights of Suzanne Wylde have been asserted. This book is presented solely for motivational purposes only. This is a work of fiction. Any resemblance to actual events or persons, living or dead, is entirely coincidental.

www.suzannewylde.com

I am perfect

You can find more colouring pages at www.suzannewylde.com and in the Perfect activity book.

www.ingramcontent.com/pod-product-compliance
Lightning Source LLC
Chambersburg PA
CBHW041224240426
43661CB00012B/1133